The Country Life Picture Book of
The Thames

The Country Life Picture Book of
The Thames

Gordon Winter

COUNTRY LIFE BOOKS

frontispiece
Abingdon, one of the most beautiful old towns in
England, was the county town of Berkshire for
many centuries, until it was supplanted by Reading.
It is mainly 18th century, but retains some fine
medieval buildings.

Published by Country Life Books,
an imprint of Newnes Books,
a division of The Hamlyn Publishing Group Limited,
84-88 The Centre, Feltham, Middlesex, England
and distributed for them by
The Hamlyn Publishing Group Limited
Rushden, Northants, England

First published 1982
Second impression 1985

ISBN 0 600 36829 7

Printed in Czechoslovakia
52096

Introduction

For almost all its lifetime the Thames has gone quietly about its business of being a river; that is to say, of carrying rainwater to the sea. It has gone quietly, or run softly in Edmund Spenser's famous phrase, because it has seldom had occasion to be violent or noisy. With a fall of only some 350 feet from source to mouth (though the amount of the fall has changed over the ages and is still changing) the Thames has been able to avoid the outbreaks of violence that have marked the course of less orderly waters such as the St Lawrence or the Zambesi. It is true, however, that the Thames has not always slept in the same bed. From time to time it has stirred itself from its gentle slumber and changed its course, partly as a result of successive Ice Ages; and it has left behind it, where it previously ran, those convenient gravel terraces on which early man settled and on which much of early London was built.

At a very early stage in its history the Thames was merely a tributary of the Rhine. That, of course, was before the Channel had divided our islands from the European Continent. For most of measurable earthly time, the river has run its course without participation or interference from the hand of man, simply because there were no men about. Only in the last, small fraction of time, that is to say for the past half-million years or so, have men appeared on or near the river, and begun to make use of it. Early paleolithic flint tools, of a type known as Abbevillian, have been found at Caversham, among many other places in the Thames Valley. About 450,000 years ago, the Abbevillians are thought to have withdrawn southward away from the encroaching Ice Age, there being then no Channel, and to have been replaced by a flake-culture people known as Clactonian, from flint tools found at Clacton, which was on the bank of a former course of the Thames.

And at Swanscombe, in Kent, lived, about 250,000 years ago, the occupant of the human skull that ranks as the earliest surviving fragments of *Homo sapiens sapiens* in these islands.

All these and later peoples were hunter-gatherers, living on what they could kill or find. The first primitive herdsmen and farmers did not appear until as recently as 4,000 BC, probably crossing the Channel in vessels of skin and wood, somewhat like the surviving Irish curraghs or Welsh coracles, or perhaps in 'extended' dugouts, and making their way up the Thames estuary. Those primitive craft were the forerunners of all our present-day boats on the river; and with the neolithic farmers and herdsmen the modern history of the Thames can be considered to have begun. From that time on, the story of the Thames is to a large extent the story of England.

Thames water, it is often said, is liquid history. The facts of geography have made that inevitable. When most of the country was either forest or swamp, rivers provided the easiest form of transport, as they did in Canada until very recently; and the Thames led from the Continent of Europe right into the heart of England. Long before the Romans came, the Thames was our principal inland trading route. It was also the only serious water barrier in the southern half of the island, for those trying to travel either north or south; and its fords, and later its bridges, were always of strategic importance. Just as for centuries the Rhine divided Europe, so in Alfred's day the Thames marked the southern limit of the Danelaw.

But it is as a highway and trading route that the Thames has made its greatest contribution to our history; indeed it remained our principal trading route, at least as far as London, until the middle of the present century. Those reading this Introduction may like to reflect that they happen to be alive at the first moment in the whole of English history when the Thames above Tilbury has lost its vital status as a trading highway. Father Thames has, in effect, been forced to accept early retirement; not just early but premature, because it is by no means improbable that we shall recover from our present obsession with road transport and return to making better commercial use, as our Continental neighbours do, of

our elaborate system of canals and waterways, with
which, of course, the Thames is linked. Our failure to
make commercial use of the Thames and our other
inland waterways is the stranger when it is
remembered that in Britain we have an advantage
denied to our Continental competitors: our
waterways are joined not only internally, but by the
sea around us, which provides a natural maritime
ring-road.

Though it is true that man has shaped the landscape
in the Thames Valley, it is also true that the landscape,
by the facts of geography, has moulded the history of
man. But because man, through pre-history and
most of history, lived mainly on the gravel, recent
quarrying or building development has removed a
large part of the evidence. We know, for example,
that there were neolithic causewayed camps at
Abingdon and at Staines, destroyed in recent years.
Simularly there were important henges, neolithic
religious centres, at Dorchester and Stanton Harcourt,
both lost to gravel quarrying, and there must have
been many others. Some of them, at least, can be
made out from the faint imprint that is still visible in
aerial photographs.

Neolithic farmers would not have found it easy to
work the fertile but marshy land, or land frequently
flooded, in the Thames Valley; they preferred the
uplands, and especially the chalk hills within reach of
so much of the upper Thames. By about 2,500 BC the
first metal-workers, known as the Beaker people
from their characteristic pottery, made their way up
the river, bringing with them the technology that
gradually replaced the Stone Age in Britain; though
the Stone Age, which has left its imprint on our
inherited memories stretched over much the longest
part of prehistory, did not end suddenly, and its
influence on our habits has not entirely ended yet. A
highly skilled bronze technology grew up along the
course of the Thames, and evidence of the wealthy
and settled civilisation that developed is provided by
bronze swords, spears, axes, ornaments and many

other artefacts found near the river or in the river bed
itself. It is not improbable that as much waits to be
recovered from the river as has already been found.

About 700 BC, iron began to appear, a more easily
found and cheaper alternative to bronze. The iron-
workers came up the Thames, like so many of their
predecessors, from the Continent, and some of the
finds near the river are reminders of how high the
standards of craftsmanship were, judged by our own.
But iron is a highly perishable material, more so than
either bronze or stone, and the most durable
memorials of the Iron Age are the hill-forts found all
over southern Britain, and in the Thames Valley at
Uffington and Wittenham Clumps among many
other places, including suburban St George's Hill.

By the time Caesar made his crossing of the Thames
in 54 BC (he did not tell us where; possible guesses are
Brentford or Westminster) much of the Thames
Valley had probably begun to look recognisably like
the countryside we know today. When the Claudian
invasion of AD 43 added towns and roads, the two
major Roman contributions to the landscape, more of
the present pattern was permanently set. London
became not only the capital but the major sea-port
that it has been ever since; and the Romans left
important river-ports as well, notably Staines and
Dorchester, which have not kept pace with changing
needs. It is arguable that the Roman centuries reduced
the importance of the Thames, because Roman roads
partially took over from it as a commercial and
administrative highway. Nevertheless the Romans
appreciated the advantages of living and farming in
the Thames catchment area, and have left an
abudance of farm and villa sites as evidence, two of the
most notable being at Ditchley, which is calculated to
have been the farmhouse of a 500-acre holding; and at
Chedworth, in the Coln Valley near Cirencester,
which is a good place to see how a rich country
landowner lived in the 3rd century AD.

After the departure of the Legions, and the defeat of
Arthur and other Romano-British leaders by the

Molesey lock, just below Taggs Island and opposite Hampton Court.

incoming Saxons, the Roman roads fell into disrepair (imagine what would happen to our own motorway system, after 50 years without maintenance) and the Thames resumed its role as the principal highway in and out of the capital. In this Introduction I do not propose to say more about the importance of the river in government and commerce from Saxon times onward, because most readers will be aware of it already, and many books have been written about it. The long list of surviving royal and episcopal palaces that line the banks is sufficient evidence, and many of them appear in the photographs that follow. Moreover from Alfred to Elizabeth II is only eleven centuries, that is to say the allotted span of no more than 16 men taken consecutively. That is a mere blink of an eye in the time scale of the Thames, so to dwell at length on those few recent years would be disproportionate. It is better to consider the Thames as a whole, over the entire length of man's habitation of the Thames Valley. Only then can we see it as a permanent and enduring entity, which will survive the worst that industrial man can do to it. When industrial man withdraws, as the Legions withdrew, the Thames will still be there, uniquely gentle and uniquely beautiful.

J. D. C. Pellow put it well in his poem, 'After London'.

> London Bridge is broken down;
> Green is the grass on Ludgate Hill;
> I know a farmer in Camden Town
> Killed a brock by Pentonville.
>
> I have heard my grandam tell
> How some thousand years ago
> Houses stretched from Camberwell
> Right to Highbury and Bow.
>
> Down by Shadwell's golden meads
> Tall ships' masts would stand as thick
> As the pretty, tufted reeds
> That the Wapping children pick.

Pellow wrote those prescient lines in 1923, and already, only 60 years later, the forest of ships' masts, once characteristic of the Port of London, has vanished.

When I was a young man in the 1930s I spent much of my leisure rowing on the Thames as a member of London Rowing Club at Putney. In those days, if you fell out of a boat, or if the boat sank, the principal risk was not drowning but typhoid. We used to boast that the Thames was the world's largest navigable sewer. That was not far from the truth. Yet until the middle of the 19th century the water appears to have been surprisingly clean. It was common for the rich and the great to swim in London's river without ill-effect. In the 18th-century there is a record, in one of Lord Chesterfield's letters, that the Earl of Pembroke swam at Whitehall regularly. And Byron boasted that he swam all the way from Westminster to London Bridge, considerably further and colder than his more famous swim across the Hellespont. What made the Tideway so filthy in the middle and latter part of the 19th century was not simply the increasing population and industrialisation of the capital. It was something sudden and dramatic, which was done, oddly enough, with the intention of improving hygenic conditions. To understand what happened it is necessary to look back a little.

London's population doubled between about the beginning and the end of the 18th century, and that in itself began to cause problems in the disposal of human waste. The existing drains were intended to cope only with rainwater, and in theory, at least, were not supposed to carry sewage. Earth closets were common, and their contents removed at night and carried out of the city on carts, where it was used, and indeed valued, as fertiliser, particularly for the market gardens on the outskirts of the city. Other house closets drained into individual or communal cesspools. Then, at the beginning of the 19th century, water-closets began to come into fashion. The first Duke of Wellington was immensely proud of the water-closets that he installed at Stratfield Saye, some of which can still be seen. The effect on London's sewage disposal, however, was disastrous. The water-closets and cesspools over-flowed into the drains, and then into the Thames.

In 1843 a new body, the Metropolitan Commissioners of Sewers, was set up. One of its first actions was to do away with individual and communal cesspools, and insist that all the households concerned should be attached to new sewers, which drained into the Thames. At the time it was thought that this would improve sanitation in the poorer parts of London. Not surprisingly the Thames could not cope. It had been hoped that the raw sewage would be carried by the river to the sea; what actually happened was that most of it simply floated up and down with the tide.

In 1855 the Metropolitan Board of Works was established, and set about the task of cleaning up the mess. A scheme was worked out to build a number of large new sewers, which would carry the contents of London's drains some ten miles down-river to a new outfall at Barking, which, it was reckoned, was far enough away to prevent the sewage from coming upstream again on the tide. This plan required legislation, and by the time the Bill came before Parliament, in 1858, the stench from the river, as it flowed past the Palace of Westminster, was so bad that sheets were hung up in the House, soaked in disinfectant, in an attempt to smother the smell.

Needless to say the 1858 scheme, though it worked within the area of London for a time, merely passed the problem on to those unfortunate enough to be living further downstream. It was not until years later that the sewage was treated before it was discharged. Meanwhile new factories were continually adding to the industrial pollution of London's river.

The effect of all this, in the 19th century and well into the present century, on the fish in the Thames is not hard to imagine. It was impossible for fish to live, and the total absence of fish life continued until the early 1950s. Yet in previous ages the Thames had been a constant and valued source of fish for Londoners and others who lived along its banks. In the 16th century Holinshead, in his *Chronicles*, wrote in glowing terms of Thames salmon, and there are many references to salmon, together with other fish, being plentiful. At one time more than 3,000 Thames salmon were sent to market in a season. Billingsgate itself became a fish-market because it was originally where fish caught in the Thames were brought ashore.

Above the Tideway, pollution never became so completely out of control, largely because of the good work of the Thames Conservancy, set up in 1857. In 1909 control of pollution below Teddington weir was made the responsibility of the Port of London Authority, but it was not until 1974 that pollution control of the whole of the Thames catchment area was again placed under a single management, the Thames Water Authority.

Today the tidal Thames can boast that it is the cleanest metropolitan estuary in the world. That happy state of affairs is the result of a 20-year programme by all the authorities involved, combined with co-operation from the industries that had previously discharged noxious waste into the river. The fresh-water Thames remains, as it has long been, well stocked with fish, though a new danger has recently been identified – lead poisoning of swans from lead weights used by anglers.

The success in bringing the Tideway back to life is well illustrated by a leaflet, recently published by the TWA, which lists a total of 97 species of fish recorded in the river. Of that number, 90 species were found in the three-year period up to December 1977, by TWA biologists conducting routine surveys of river life between Kew and Tilbury. The tally includes sole, lemon sole, plaice, whiting, mullet, red mullet, herring and cod, and in many species the numbers are high.

By 1975 the TWA considered that the whole of the

Dusk on the Embankment near the Hungerford Bridge. On the left is the French–chateau–like building of Whitehall Court and in the distance is the Post Office Tower.

Thames was now becoming clean enough to justify an attempt to re-introduce salmon. The attempt began with pilot releases of eggs, parr and smolts, mostly in the nursery streams in the Cotswolds and Chilterns, the object being to test survival in a Thames environment. The tests went well, and in the late 1970s it was decided that the water would be clean enough for smolts to make their way down to the sea and for adult salmon to return. After consultation with the many authorities involved, the TWA decided on a seven-year programme, to begin in 1979. The plan was to release at least 50,000 parr or smolts annually, and this was done between March and May, 1979. Two full-time scientists were appointed to check the progress of the experiment. A proportion of all young stock were marked to facilitate identification.

Introduction of young stock continued during 1980 and 1981, and 1981 saw the first significant return of adult fish. In the late summer of that year eight adult salmon were taken from the river between the Tideway and Reading, and of the eight, three bore identifiable marks, clearly establishing that these were fish that had gone down the river as smolts and were returning from the sea as salmon. At the same time salmon were seen jumping weirs at Shepperton and Sunbury. As this book goes to press it is known that the TWA intends to build a salmon pass at Molesey weir, both to help salmon on their way up river and to provide a check on their numbers. At long last it looks as though the Thames is again a salmon river.

It is of course true that the cleaning up of the Tideway has been made easier by the decline of London's 19th-century docks. The full extent of that decline can best be shown by the fall in employment levels. In 1964, the year in which the Port of London achieved its highest-ever tonnage of goods, 61.3 million tons, there were 11,948 Port of London Authority employees. Of those, 3,942 were registered dock workers. By the end of 1980 the total of PLA employees had fallen to 6,670, of whom 3,754 were

registered dock workers. But throughout the port, and not taking PLA employment figures only, the total of registered dock workers fell from 24,972 in 1964 to only 5,779 by the end of 1980.

That, however, must not be taken to indicate the decline of London as one of the world's greatest sea-ports. What has happened is that the business of the port has moved down the estuary, as river-ports have always tended to do. Recognising, some twenty years ago, the changes in cargo-handling techniques brought about by containerisation, the PLA began to invest heavily in Tilbury Docks, some twenty-five miles downstream of London Bridge. Before 1960, Tilbury Docks handled less than half a million tonnes a year. A large dock-basin constructed there in the mid-1960s, and the opening of a new riverside container berth in 1978, have multiplied the capacity more than tenfold. Today Tilbury handles general cargo and passenger cruise ships, but the bulk of its trade is made up of lift-on/lift-off containers and roll-on/roll-off traffic. At the same time the Victoria deep-water container terminal, just upstream from Greenwich, has recently completed a major construction programme and more than doubled its capacity.

In other words, employment in the Port of London has declined because the business of the port has changed from being labour-intensive to being capital-intensive. Londoners can no longer stand on London Bridge and watch ships discharging their cargoes in the Upper Pool. Nevertheless the lower estuary remains a great artery serving the commercial heart of Britain, and the Port of London is still Britain's premier port. In 1980, in spite of world recession, it handled 48 million tonnes. All general cargo that would once have gone to the India and Millwall Docks and Royal Docks has been transferred to Tilbury, though the PLA's bulk wine terminal remains in the India and Millwall Docks, handling between seven and ten million gallons of wine a year. So to the success story of the cleaning up of London's

Tilbury Docks. Though the 18th- and 19th-century docks and wharves below Tower Bridge have lost their traffic, London remains Britain's premier port. What has happened is that cargo that would once have gone to the India, Millwall and Royal Docks has moved twenty-five miles down-river to Tilbury, where the Port of London Authority has developed a new port with facilities for roll-on/roll-off and container traffic. Tilbury handled 48 million tonnes of cargo in 1980, and is still growing.

river can be added a parallel success story of the redevelopment of the Port of London, to keep abreast of modern needs.

The rebuilding of London's docks is not the only major construction that has been taking place on the Tideway. Equally important, perhaps more important, is the immense engineering task of building the Thames Barrier at Woolwich, which is due to be in operation by December, 1982.

A number of factors have combined to make the Thames Barrier necessary. Sea levels all round Britain have been rising compared with land levels, probably as a result of the melting of the polar ice cap. At the same time the land surface of south-eastern England has gradually been sinking. This has to be borne in mind when we wonder how Caesar's army could possibly have forded the Thames at either Westminster or Brentford. It was feasible, we must suppose, not only because the river had not been embanked, and so was spread over a wider, shallower area; but because the water level of the tidal river was generally lower, and the land level of the river-bed was higher. It is reckoned that mean sea level at London Bridge is now 3.5 metres above what it was in Roman times.

As it happens, accurate records of the level of the Thames in London have been kept for nearly 200 years, and from these records it is clear that the tide observed at London Bridge has been growing steadily higher. The critical danger arises from a predictable very high tide, in spring or autumn, occurring at the same time as a tidal surge, that is to say a moment when gales in the North Sea force an abnormal volume of water into the funnel of the Thames estuary. As is now widely understood, if that should happen before the Thames Barrier is completed, more than 45 square miles along the shores of the Thames below Richmond might be flooded, and more than one million Londoners would be put at risk. As I write this Introduction, there are still two danger periods to be passed before

the expected completion date at the end of 1982. It is calculated that when the Barrier is finished it will have cost more than £400 million; but compared with what would inevitably happen without it, as the sea continues to rise and the land to fall, it will be cheap at the price.

In former centuries the Thames in and near London was alive with boats, pulled by watermen and lightermen, which played a role in London's transport akin to that of cars and taxis, buses and lorries today. Watermen carried passengers; lightermen carried goods. Yet today their traditions survive only in the Company of Watermen and Lightermen; and the men who navigate the power-driven pleasure boats that carry tourists on the Tideway are still Freemen of that ancient Company.

The Thames watermen, for many centuries, rowed the private barges of the rich and powerful, and provided a taxi service for ordinary citizens who wanted to cross the river where there were no bridges, or to travel up and down it. The service offered by the watermen was not without its hazards, and crossing the Thames in the 16th century was probably at least as dangerous as crossing the Strand in the 20th. In 1514, in the reign of Henry VIII, Parliament found it necessary to pass an Act to regulate fares for given distances by water, but evidently that did not diminish the number of accidents. In 1555 a further Bill was laid before Parliament referring to 'many misfortunes chancing of late years to a great number of the King's and Queen's subjects . . . by reason of rude, ignorant and unskilful watermen'.

On of the traditional hardships of the life of a London waterman was his particular liability to be impressed to serve in the Navy. That was no doubt a compliment to his renowned toughness and skill. London watermen are said to have been preferred by Nelson whenever he could get them. I referred earlier, however, to having spent much of my youth rowing in eights and fours up and down the Tideway;

and London's amateur oarsmen can well claim to be the successors of the professional watermen of Nelson's day. So it was with distinct relief that I discovered, when not long ago I was given the honour of being made a Freeman of the City of London, that one of the privileges of a Freeman is that he cannot be impressed to serve in the Navy.

Though it is possible to take a boat all the way from Lechlade to London along the Thames, it is not possible to walk the same distance along the banks of the river. This is primarily because, although there is a public right of navigation on the river, there is no public right of way along the towpath except where it is also a footpath. Along some stretches of the river there is no access at all, and the walker has to make his way across country and rejoin the river further down. Moreover the towpath itself keeps changing from one side of the river to the other. That originally happened whenever a landowner on one bank objected to a towpath on his land. In the days of horse-drawn barges the difficulty was overcome by the establishment of ferry boats, capable of carrying horses, where it was necessary for the horse to be taken across. Needless to say, those ferries no longer operate; and the would-be Thames walker may have to go a long distance out of his way in order to cross by a bridge.

Many people, and especially the Ramblers' Association, have been trying for several years to persuade the multiplicity of authorities and riparian owners to co-operate in the completion of a Thames Walk all the way along the river. The Ramblers Association publishes a guide to the 156-mile walk that can be made from the source to Putney, allowing for detours; and an admirable River Thames Map, published by Stanford's, shows footpaths, although it is primarily intended for those who travel by water. The Countryside Commission recently instituted a study of a proposed Thames long-distance footpath, following the river all the way, and financed a project officer, employed by the TWA, to walk the course

and identify problem areas. The Countryside Commission expects his draft report by the spring of 1982.

We who enjoy the river in the 1980s are indebted to generations of landowners and farmers, as well as to the Thames Conservancy (now TWA) and the local authorities, for ensuring that for much the greatest part of its length the Thames runs through a well-farmed and unspoiled valley of exceptional peace and beauty. All of us know of eyesores that should not be there: for example, a car plant near Runnymede, of all places, that should never have been allowed through the planning net. Happily, however, such mistakes remind us of how much worse things might easily have been.

Some of us think that the amenity of the river is at present in danger from too many power-boats. There is no maximum number of power-boats that may be licensed as pleasure-craft, and the official view is that no top limit is necessary. My personal opinion is that a top limit is essential for a waterway as sensitive as the Thames, and that the sooner it is fixed, the better. As petrol becomes scarcer and more expensive we shall no doubt see a revival of electric launches, which are quieter and less smelly than petrol or diesel craft. But too many power-boats of any kind destroy the tranquility that each individual boat-owner is looking for.

The Thames is the inheritance of all of us who know it and love it. It must not be dominated by any single group or interest. Only by constant care and determination will its unique qualities be preserved.

Thameshead in Trewsbury Mead, some three miles
west of Cirencester, Gloucestershire. Here is the
officially recognised source of the Thames, though
the spring is visible only in winter. Seven Springs,
near Cheltenham, the rival claimant, is
acknowledged as the source of the Churn, a
tributary of the Thames.

Father Thames. For many years he reclined,
appropriately, at Thameshead, but vandalism led to
his removal to safer quarters at St John's lock near
Lechlade, the first lock on the river.

The lusty infant Thames at Ashton Keynes, between Thameshead and St John's lock. Ashton Keynes, and its sister settlement, Somerford Keynes just above it, are the first villages on the river and have been there, and flourished because of the Thames, at least since Saxon times. The water is navigable here in a canoe, as no doubt it once was in a dugout, but it is not officially open to navigation above Lechlade.

A footbridge at Cricklade (*top*), where the Churn
joins the Thames. Cricklade also boasts a more
impressive stone bridge, where the Roman road,
now the A419, crosses.

Castle Eaton church (*above*), on the Wiltshire bank,
downstream of Cricklade. Its name is the first
nominal reminder of the long list of fortified places
that have guarded crossings of the Thames, or
themselves been guarded by the river.

Young successors of the early Britons explore the waterway at Inglesham, just above Lechlade. Their craft, though similar in size to the dugouts in which their remote forebears explored the same stretch of water, are however modelled on Eskimo kayaks, confusingly known in England as canoes.

Buscot Park, two miles south-east of Lechlade. The
Adam style is misleading, because the house is the
result of skilful restoration by the second Lord
Faringdon, in the 1930s, of a house built in the 1780s
but greatly altered by the Victorians. Buscot House,
with nearly 4,000 acres, is now owned by the
National Trust. Among the notable contents is the
series of Pre-Raphaelite pictures in the saloon, *The
Legend of the Briar Rose*, by Burne-Jones.

St John's lock at Lechlade, where the Leach joins the Thames, 123 miles above the Tideway.

The pointed arches of the medieval 'new' bridge (*right*), spanning both the Thames and its tributary, the Windrush, at Newbridge. On the far side is the excellent inn, The Rose Revived. There seems to be no convincing account of the origin of that name, unless perhaps it refers to the 'rosy wreath' that Ben Jonson sent to Celia, and which was restored because she breathed on it.

Kelmscott Manor (*above*), some two miles below Buscot. It retains much of the dream quality that attracted William Morris to make his home there from 1871 until his death in 1896, and which he described in a letter as 'a heaven on earth'. The serenity of heaven was disturbed for a while by the strained relations between William, his wife Jane, and Dante Gabriel Rossetti, who lived there in a kind of *ménage à trois* from 1871 to 1874, when Rossetti left. The exact nature of that *ménage* is uncertain but may be known when letters between them become available in 1988.

Swinford toll bridge (*below*) by Eynsham lock. The
bridge was built by the Earl of Abingdon in 1777 and
remains one of the two bridges over the Thames
where tolls are still charged; the other is at
Whitchurch. The toll-house, on the Eynsham side
of the river, displays an early list of prices.

The old paddle-weir at Northmoor lock (*opposite,
top*), two miles below Newbridge. The moor on the
north-west side of the river, to which the name
refers, was once marshy land on what is almost an
island between the Windrush and a bend in the
Thames. Paddle-weirs were designed so that they
could be opened to let traffic through, before the
invention of locks.

The Ferry Inn at Bablock Hythe (*opposite, bottom*),
below Northmoor lock. Here it was that Matthew
Arnold wrote of the Scholar Gypsy crossing the
stripling Thames, and 'Trailing in the cool stream thy
fingers wet, As the slow punt swings round'.

Near Oxford (*right*). The impact of modern industry on the river is mercifully small.

The Trout Inn at Godstow (*below*) on the edge of Oxford. On the opposite side of the river from the Trout are the ruins of Godstow nunnery, where Henry II is said to have met the young woman who became his mistress, Fair Rosamund, daughter of Lord Clifford. The lines on the sundial are from *The Rubáiyát* of Omar Khayyám.

This plaque at Swinford (*above*) provides a fitting memorial to the long years when the Thames above Teddington weir was in the good care of the Thames Conservancy, to which all lovers of the river are indebted, and which is now merged in the Thames Water Authority.

Oxford: the Radcliffe Camera (*top*), by James Gibb, 1737–49. Hawksmoor was one of the unsuccessful applicants for the work, initiated when Dr Radcliffe left to the University the then immense sum of £40,000 for a new library building.

The Botanic Garden, Oxford (*above*). Founded in the 17th century for the cultivation of plants used in herbal medicine, it now covers a much wider scientific and educational purpose.

Magdalen College, Oxford. Founded by the Bishop
of Winchester in 1458, many of Magdalen's buildings
are 15th century, but the New Buildings, seen here
beyond the bridge over the Cherwell, were the work
of William Townesend in 1733. Because they are
not typical of university buildings, they narrowly
escaped being gothicized in the early 19th century by
a generation that did not admire their classical
simplicity.

Tom Tower, Christ Church, Oxford (*opposite*). This college, founded by Wolsey in 1525, was originally called Cardinal College. The mixture of styles of Tom Tower is the result of Wren adding a tower on top of Wolsey's gateway, though Wren intended to 'agree with the founder's work' and avoid 'an unhandsome medley'. Beyond the arch is Tom Quad, the largest of all the Oxford quads.

Punts on the river (*above*). The universities of Oxford and Cambridge hold opposite opinions concerning which is the bow of a punt and which the stern. At Oxford the punter stands in the well of the punt, as in this photograph; at Cambridge he stands on the deck. It is probable that punting is not now as significant in the social life of undergraduates as it was to the contemporaries of Zuleika Dobson, before young men and women had easy access to motor-cars.

Rowing at Oxford. The river at Oxford (like the
Cam at Cambridge) is not wide or straight enough,
over a long enough distance, for eights to race
abreast. For that reason, the tradition of bumping
races has developed, in which crews are grouped in
divisions, and each college boat tries to catch and
bump the boat in front of it. Next day they start
again in their new order. The college first boat which
has 'gone Head', or remained Head of the River,
starts again in that position next year. At Oxford
these races are called Torpids in the spring and
Eights Week in the summer; the Cambridge
equivalents are Lents and May Week.

The west front of St Mary's, Iffley, one of the most celebrated of Norman churches, though the rose window is Victorian. Pevsner rates it as one of the best preserved 12th-century village churches in England. Iffley, though once a village, is now a suburb of Oxford. Its lock was originally built in the 17th century, and is one of the first three locks, or pound-locks to give them their full name, constructed on the Thames. The others are at Abingdon and Sandford.

Nuneham House, five miles below Iffley. The original Palladian mansion was built in 1756 by the first Lord Harcourt, but there are additions made in 1832 and later. The park is the work of Capability Brown and William Mason. Nuneham Park is owned by the University of Oxford and is open to the public on certain days during the summer. On the opposite side of the river is the boathouse of Radley College, a distinguished rowing school.

Nuneham Courtenay village is a notable example of
an 18th-century model village, built at a discreet
distance from Lord Harcourt's great house and the
park. It replaced the old village built nearer the river,
the occupants of which were, to use modern jargon,
re-housed. Here, as everywhere along the Thames, is
much evidence of prehistoric occupation, and at
nearby Sandford bronze-age daggers, a sword and a
spear were found in the river-bed and are now in the
British Museum. No doubt there are many others
waiting to be dredged out.

Sutton Courtenay. Unplanned houses span many centuries, in sharp contrast with Nuneham Courtenay.

Abingdon. The 17th- and 18th-century almshouses
stand round St Helen's church, the spire of which can
be seen. The almshouses are among many splendid
buildings in this mainly 18th-century market town.
Built on the outer side of a sharp bend in the river,
Abingdon has attracted continuous human
settlement since the early Stone Age, and its story is a
kind of potted history of England. The abbey dates
from the 7th century.

Abingdon: the Old Gaol. This building, which
dominates the Abingdon reach of the river, was
built during the Napoleonic Wars, but has recently
been adapted as a recreation centre. Its exterior,
softened by time and careful planting, no longer
suggests the grim hardship it must once have imposed
on its prisoners, but it stands in a town of
exceptionally fine and gentle buildings, notably the
17th-century County Hall in the market square.

Clifton Hampden (*below*). As the name tells us, the main part of the village stands above the Thames, on a cliff. It is known for its thatched cottages, irreverently described by Pevsner as 'tea-cosy cottages'. At the Barley Mow Inn here Jerome K. Jerome wrote part of *Three Men in a Boat*, and describes the Barley Mow as 'the quaintest, most old-world inn up the river'.

The White Hart at Dorchester (*right*). Dorchester was for centuries one of the most important towns in the whole of the Thames Valley. Commanding the junction of the Thame and the Thames, and protected on three sides by those rivers, it has neolithic and Bronze Age monuments, an Iron Age fort, and, as the name tells us, was a Roman fortified town. Its importance continued into the Middle Ages. Now its principal industries appear to be hotels and antique shops.

Sunset over the river at Long Wittenham (*right*). The Wittenhams are – or were – particularly rich in Saxon finds. Long Wittenham, on the Saxon side when the Thames was the southern boundary of the Danelaw, had a pagan Saxon cemetery, but in it was found the Long Wittenham Stoup, a wooden bucket sheathed in bronze with Christian decoration, now in the British Museum. Industrial Age man, a recent arrival, seems to have added only pollution.

The Abbey Church of St Peter and St Paul, Dorchester (*above*), all that is left of the town's former magnificence. At the Dissolution the Abbey church, like that of Tewkesbury in Gloucestershire, was saved by the townspeople and maintained as their parish church, when almost all the rest of the monastic buildings were pulled down. Its most celebrated feature is the Jesse window, a brilliant medieval combination of stone and glass, in which the stone figures are designed to spring from the body of Jesse. The original abbey gatehouse became the local school and is now a museum. The present lych-gate leading into the High Street is by Butterfield, 1852. Most of the prehistoric finds from Dorchester are now in the Ashmolean Museum at Oxford.

Wittenham Clumps (*below*). The two hills, known as Sinodun Hills, or Wittenham Clumps, are widely noticed for their trees, but much their most important feature is the Iron Age hill–fort, clearly seen in the photograph. If this fort, and the Iron Age fort on the Dorchester side of the Thames immediately opposite, were in the same hands, they would have commanded the river and controlled all its traffic. It is a reasonable guess that that was their purpose.

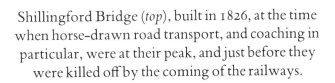

Shillingford Bridge (*top*), built in 1826, at the time when horse-drawn road transport, and coaching in particular, were at their peak, and just before they were killed off by the coming of the railways.

In the coaching era Benson (*above*) on the old road between Oxford and Henley, was renowned for its inns. The Castle Inn has the original wrought-iron frame for its sign.

Wallingford Bridge. The curious bridge with a total of seventeen arches is medieval in origin but was rebuilt in 1809, with the balustrade typical of that time. Wallingford, one of England's oldest royal boroughs, is, like Dorchester and Abingdon, yet another example of a town that grew to great importance because of its position on the Thames, and in this case because of its ford, but has since declined. At the time of Domesday it was probably bigger than Cambridge, Chester or Exeter. Its more recent importance is indicated by the splendid Town Hall of 1670 and, by St Peters, of 1777, with an open-work spire. At the Dissolution, Wallingford's monastery helped to pay for Wolsey's Cardinal College, now Christ Church, Oxford.

The Penny Farthing shop at Crowmarsh Gifford.
The three Crowmarsh hamlets are on the eastern
side of the river across Wallingford Bridge. Grim's
Ditch, a prehistoric earthwork here, is one of the
innumerable linear earthworks or ditches in Britain,
about which little is known with certainty;
they may have been defensive, or dug to mark
boundaries, or both.

Wildflowers by the river near Moulsford. The Beetle and Wedge at Moulsford is said to be the model for the Potwell Inn in H. G. Wells's novel, *The History of Mr Polly*. Alfred Polly, approaching the inn on a hot day in May, whispers to himself: '"Provender . . . cold sirloin for choice, and nutbrown brew and wheaten bread" . . . the nearer he came to the place the more he liked it'. He immediately took on, with no experience, the vacant job of ferryman at the inn.

The Magdalen College barge, come to rest at Goring.
It has what is claimed to be the first concrete hull in
England. The Goring Gap, where the Thames
makes its way between the chalk hills of the
Chilterns and the Berkshire Downs, is generally
considered to offer the most spectacular scenery on
the river, spectacular not being an adjective often
applied to the gentle Thames. From far into
prehistoric times, the ford here provided the vital
link between the Icknield Way and the Ridgeway,
on the Berkshire side, and was therefore one of the
most important fords in Britain. The Ridgeway,
however, had an alternative crossing a few miles
further down at Pangbourne.

The twin towns of Goring in Oxfordshire and
Streatley in Berkshire, seen from the Berkshire
Downs. From Goring to Henley the Thames runs
through the Chilterns Area of Outstanding Natural
Beauty, which includes the Chiltern beechwoods,
and is in the joint care of the local authorities and the
Countryside Commission.

Goring lock (*top*). This lock, with its well kept gardens, would excite attention anywhere else in the world. Here it is taken for granted – a tribute to the Thames lock-keepers and to the high standards set by the Thames Conservancy.

Basildon Park (*above*). Built in Bath stone by John Carr for Sir Francis Sykes in 1776, it is rated by Pevsner as 'the most splendid Georgian mansion of Berkshire'.

The mill at Mapledurham, one of the oldest surviving corn-mills on the Thames. The area of Mapledurham has remained mercifully unspoilt in spite of being on the outskirts of Reading. The river here, moreover, runs through *Wind in the Willows* country. Kenneth Grahame spent the last years of his life just upstream at Pangbourne/Whitchurch and it was to this reach that E. H. Shephard came to find the right setting for his illustrations to *The Wind in the Willows*. So sharp-eyed watermen can expect to find Mole on the bank, or Rat in the water, whenever they mess about in boats in these parts.

Mapledurham House. Built from 1585 for Sir
Richard Blount, it is one of the most distinguished
Elizabethan houses on the Thames. Alexander Pope,
who visited the house, regarded absence from
London as an affliction. He wrote, about a
Miss Blount of his day:

She went, to plain-work, and to purling brooks,
Old-fashioned halls, dull aunts and croaking rooks.
She went from opera, park, assembly, play,
To morning walks, and prayers three hours a day.

Deanery Garden, Sonning, built by Lutyens in 1901
for Edward Hudson, the founder and proprietor of
Country Life. The house stands in Thames Street, and
it was an existing wall of this street that formed the
starting point for the design. Hudson wrote in 1903 :
'So naturally has the house been planned that it seems
to have grown out of the landscape'. The garden is
one of many successful collaborations between
Lutyens and Gertrude Jekyll.

Ponies on the bank at Wargrave (*below*). In the churchyard here is the grave of Thomas Day, a barrister who wrote the children's book, *Sandford and Merton* in the 1780s, on the theme that it paid to be good. It paid Thomas Day, because the book was very successful.

Near Reading (*bottom*). Reading, known for its industries and its university, has a Victorian prison, immortalised in Wilde's *Ballad of Reading Gaol*.

The Angel at Henley-on-Thames (*below*). This
grouping of the inn, the 16th-century tower of
St Mary's church, and the bridge of 1786, is one of
the best-known Thames scenes. On the bridge are
carved stone heads representing the Thames and the
Isis, by Horace Walpole's friend, Anne Damer, who
inherited Strawberry Hill from him.

Henley during regatta week (*right*). Henley Royal
Regatta is rowed upstream over a two-lane straight
course of 1 mile 550 yards, from just below Temple
Island to just below Leander Club. Racing takes
place throughout four days, Thursday, Friday,
Saturday and Sunday, and the Saturday is always the
first in July. The regatta began in 1839.

Henley Regatta: a race just after the start, passing
Temple Island. The regatta, besides being the most
celebrated in the world, can justly claim to be rowed
over the most beautiful course. The Temple on the
island was designed by James Wyatt in 1771, as part
of the planned view from nearby Fawley Court, the
gardens of which were being laid out at the time by
Capability Brown.

Spectators: a traditional element in the Henley
scenery. It is part of the mystique of Henley that the
Royal Regatta continues to be successful financially,
and to attract spectators as well as the world's
oarsmen by maintaining its own high standards of
management and manners. Yet the course has only
two lanes, and is longer than the Olympic distance of
2000 metres, for which top international crews
normally train.

Hambleden Mill, by Hambleden weir; a group described by the uneffusive Pevsner as 'delightful'.

Negotiating white water at Hambleden weir. Not far
away, at Bisham Abbey, below Temple lock, is a
National Sports Centre run by the Sports Council,
where canoeing is one of many river activities for
which training is available. Bisham Abbey also
incorporates the national training centre of the Lawn
Tennis Association, and has the largest artificial
grass field in Europe.

Medmenham Abbey. Some of the house is
18th-century Gothick, some of it dates from 1595.
From about 1745 Sir Francis Dashwood ran the
Hellfire Club here. The indecent painting on the
ceiling of the chapel, and the unmistakably erotic
entrance to the temple, no longer survive (they
would probably be a tourist-draw if they did); but
we have a record of what the members got up to in
Charles Johnstone's *Adventures of a Guinea*,
published between 1760 and 1765.

Marlow: the suspension bridge and the 19th-century All Saints church. The bridge, by William Tierney Clark, dates from 1831–6. Town and bridge have been protected from today's heavy traffic by a new bridge and by-pass a mile downstream. The 19th-century entrance to Marlow, shown here, is deceptive; most of the town is 18th-century and earlier, and among notable buildings is one in West Street that was formerly the Royal Military College.

Bisham Abbey is one of many examples of monastic establishments which lined the Thames from the upper reaches to the estuary, but which now survive only in name. Before the Dissolution, Bisham belonged in succession to the Templars, the Augustinians and the Benedictines. In 1553 it became the property of Sir Philip Hoby, and like his contemporaries in other parts of the country he began to rebuild it as a private house. Some of the original religious building remains, however; the great hall of the Templars survived in part as the hall of the house. Bisham Abbey is now run by the Sports Council. (*See also* page 66.)

Launching a dinghy near Cookham (*opposite, top*).

Cliveden reach (*opposite, bottom*). Cliveden, owned by the National Trust, was built by Charles Barry for the Duke of Sutherland in 1850. It was bought by the Duke of Westminster in 1870 and by the Astors in 1893. Under Lady Astor, the first woman to enter Parliament, Cliveden became a focal point of political influence. It is now the English base of Stanford University.

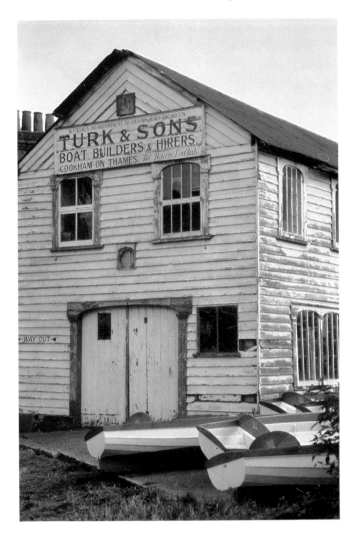

Turk and Sons' boathouse at Cookham (*above*). The Turks, like the Phelps's at Putney, have long been among the great Thames families of boat-builders. Their highly specialised skills in wooden craft, and especially in the building of racing boats for rowing, which have been passed down for generations from father to son, are now threatened by the advent of glass-reinforced plastic, which is quicker and cheaper.

Boulters lock, Maidenhead. Once crowded with pretty girls in punts; now crowded with power-boats.

Brunel's Great Western Railway bridge at Maidenhead (*below*), 1837–8. The semi-elliptical arch, 128ft wide, is claimed to be the widest brick span in the world. The spirit of the age of steam, which inspired Brunel and which, in this example, is as splendid as anything built by the Romans, also inspired Turner's depiction of the bridge in *Rain, Steam and Speed*.

The church of St Michael at Bray (*opposite*). Partly 14th century, but with many later additions. It is celebrated for its connection with the Vicar of Bray in the 18th-century song. The identity of the vicar is uncertain, but he is claimed to have been Symon Symonds, who survived at Bray through the reigns of Henry VIII, Edward VI, Mary and Elizabeth I, twice as a Protestant and twice as a Catholic. Hence the chorus:

And this is law, I will maintain
Unto my dying day, Sir:
That whatsoever King shall reign,
I'll be the Vicar of Bray, Sir.

Swan-uppers at work (*below*). From the 16th century until recently, the swan-uppers set off every July from Temple Stairs to row to Henley. Now they row from Sunbury to Pangbourne. On the way they count and mark the season's cygnets: the beaks of Dyer's cygnets with one nick; the Vintners' with two; the Sovereign's left unmarked. Swans on the Thames are threatened by lead weights left by anglers, which are picked up by the swans and poison them.

Windsor Castle (*right*), on a site of great natural strength, was begun by William the Conqueror and has been enlarged by many sovereigns since. Edward III carried out rebuilding under the care of William of Wykeham (founder of New College, Oxford, and of Winchester College). Now, covering over twelve acres, it is much the biggest castle in England and, in terms of the weapons for which it was built, among the strongest. Charles II was one of the principle rebuilders, but Windsor Castle was given its familiar outward appearance early in the 19th-century. The Round Tower in particular, though dating from Henry II, is, as we know it, the work of Wyatville, who, with his uncle, James Wyatt, also contributed much to the State Apartments. The oarsmen on the river below the Castle are the successors of the watermen who have rowed all our sovereigns, for nearly 900 years, between Windsor and London.

Royal Windsor Horse Show. The show, by gracious permission of H.M. the Queen, is held in May on the meadows by the Thames below the Castle; running through five days, it is the biggest outdoor horseshow in Britain. The Queen regularly attends and takes special interest in a number of events, notably the inter-services show-jumping. International carriage-driving championships, in which the Duke of Edinburgh takes part, are included.

The Garter Procession outside St George's Chapel,
Windsor Castle. The Order of the Garter, which was
founded by Edward III, originally used an earlier
chapel at Windsor, which stood until the 15th century
where the Albert Memorial Chapel stands now. The
present St George's Chapel was begun by Edward IV
in 1477 and was finished in 1528 by Henry VIII. The
vaulted roof rivals in splendour that of King's College
Chapel, Cambridge. The swords, helms and banners
of the Knights of the Garter hang over their stalls.
Eleven sovereigns are buried in St George's Chapel,
among them Edward IV, Henry VIII, Charles I and
George VI. Queen Victoria, however, rests in the
Royal Mausoleum at Frogmore.

The Savill Garden, Windsor Great Park. This was the first of the gardens, made in the 1930s and later, for George VI by Sir Eric Savill in Windsor Great Park. The flowering trees and shrubs are at their best in late spring, but the azaleas and rhododendrons are followed by primulas, meconopses, roses and other summer flowers. Arthur Hellyer rates it as 'one of the outstanding achievements in 20th-century garden making in Britain'.

The Nell Gwynn shop, Church Street, Windsor.
There may be some doubt whether, as is claimed, Nell
Gwynn actually lived at number 6 Church Street, but
at least she must have known it – it dates from 1640 –
and she must have passed it regularly on her way to her
home in Burford Lodge. Burford Lodge is in
St Alban's Street, named after her son, the Duke
of St Alban's. The Lodge, reconstructed, is now part
of the Royal Mews.

School Yard, Eton College. The monument is to
Henry VI, who founded Eton in 1440, under the
title: 'the King's College of Our Lady of Eton beside
Windsor'. Beyond the monument is Lupton's
Range, Lupton being the provost in the reign of
Henry VIII. The brick gatehouse dates from about
1517. Eton, and King's College, Cambridge, also
founded by Henry VI, were partly modelled on
William of Wykeham's foundations of Winchester
(1378) and New College, Oxford (1379).

Fishing at Romney Weir, Eton. To fish this weir, a
permit must be obtained from the Thames Water
Authority, and the coarse fishing includes roach, rudd,
tench, carp, perch and pike. Below the weir the
fishing from Romney Island is in the hands of Old
Windsor Angling Club. To the already good fishing
in the Thames has now been added the prospect of
salmon and salmon trout. (*See* page 12.)

The lock-keeper's house, Romney Lock. Lock-keepers on the Thames generally work the locks from 9 a.m. until dusk with, of course, off-duty periods for meals. Members of the public may operate the locks at their own risk. The rule is that a lock should be left emptying or empty, with the gates shut. Red boards are displayed at locks if an abnormally strong stream is running, when craft are advised to moor and wait. Space is provided for craft waiting to use the locks.

Runnymede. Magna Carta bears in Latin the words, over King John's seal: 'Given by our hand in the meadow that is called Runnymeade, between Windsor and Staines, on the 15th day of June in the 17th year of our reign' (1215). In the 18th century Runnymede was a racecourse. Since 1931 it has been held by the National Trust. The lodges that mark the limits of the historic ground are by Lutyens.

National 12ft dinghies at Staines. In the occasional inevitable conflict of interest between sailing, rowing, canoeing and power, sailing boats are entitled to claim right of way. The whole of the area along the Thames near Staines is now devoted to reservoirs, and to flooded gravel pits converted to water parks, so that from an aeroplane there appears to be more water than land. It was all once fertile alluvial land, however, better used for food than water.

Architectural good manners at Chertsey. Like many
small towns and villages along the river, Chertsey
has managed to retain something of the unassuming
urbanity of former centuries. Chertsey also has a fine
Georgian bridge, built of Purbeck stone in 1785, a year
before that at Henley. At Laleham, across the river,
Matthew Arnold was born in 1822. His father kept
a small school there before he became headmaster
of Rugby.

Hampton Court Palace: the West Front (*below*).
Cardinal Wolsey built his great house on land
formerly owned by the Knights of St John. The
similarity in style with the contemporary gatehouse
at Eton (page 82) is immediately apparent. Wolsey
gave the unfinished house to Henry VIII in an
unsuccessful attempt to placate him; the King
accepted the house and enlarged it. For the next two
centuries it was a favourite royal residence.

Hampton Court Palace: the East Front (*right*).
William III, who particularly enjoyed living at
Hampton Court, invited Christopher Wren to
rebuild the palace, but only the eastern side was
completed by him. It is a sombre thought that if
William had not been killed by a fall, when riding at
Hampton Court, the rebuilding would have
continued, and the whole of the Tudor palace would
have been lost. Queen Anne's fondness for Hampton
Court is remembered in Pope's couplet:

Here thou, great Anna, whom three realms obey
Dost sometimes counsel take, and sometimes tea.

Kingston Market. The Royal Borough of Kingston proudly proclaims that seven Saxon Kings were crowned here, and what is believed to be the Coronation Stone is displayed outside the Guildhall. The Italianate Town Hall of 1838 is charming, as is Kingston Bridge, of 1825. Kingston retains the conduit houses built by Wolsey to supply him with water at Hampton Court.

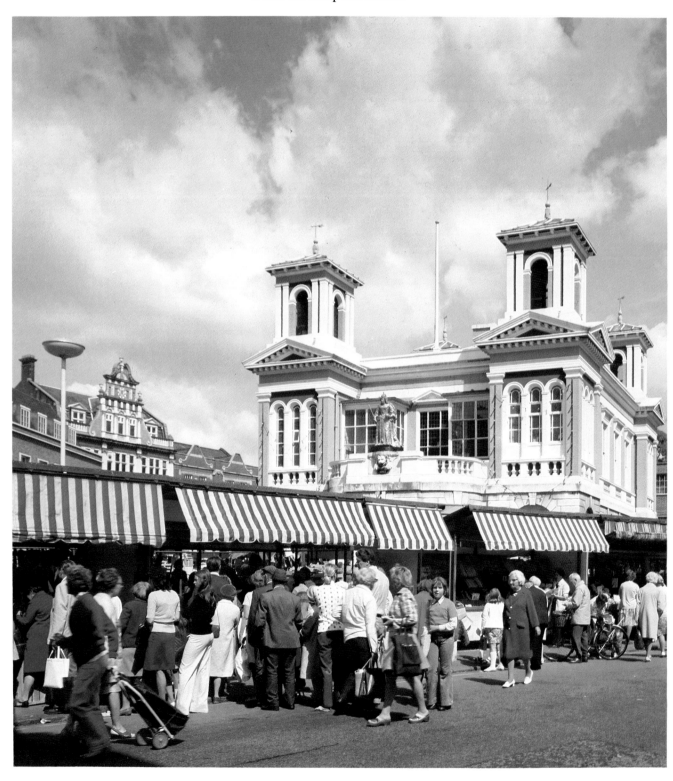

Narrow-boats at Teddington lock. Barges of this
kind, with their stylized decoration, were developed
to carry cargo on the canals rather than on the Thames.
Many of them are now maintained only as homes or
pleasure boats, but they can still be made to pay, when
time is not important. Depreciation is low compared
with lorries; and as fuel becomes more expensive,
inland-water transport, with its minimal loss of
energy from friction, is likely to become more
competitive.

Interior at Ham House, Richmond (*below*);
one of a pair of 'sleeping chayres' in original silk. The
Duke and Duchess of Lauderdale, who acquired the
house in the 17th century and filled it with splendid
things, were notoriously heartless and acquisitive.
Their faults died with them; the beauty that they
collected remains. Ham House, now owned by the
National Trust, fortunately looks much as the
Lauderdales left it.

Marble Hill House, Twickenham (*opposite, top*).
Well restored by the GLC, this Palladian villa was
built by George II for his mistress, Henrietta
Howard, a friend of Alexander Pope.

Richmond bridge and Tower House (*opposite,
bottom*). The five-arched bridge, one of the most
graceful over the Thames, was built by James Paine in
1777. Before it, there had been a horse-ferry at
Richmond – that is to say a ferry big enough to carry
horses and a carriage or cart. Paine's bridge was
sympathetically widened in 1937.

Sunset from Richmond Hill (*below*). The view from Richmond Hill has long been admired and was much painted during the 18th and 19th centuries. Richmond has had royal associations for centuries. Sheen Palace, as it was called in the Middle Ages, was rebuilt as Richmond Palace by Henry VII, who gave it that name because he had been Earl of Richmond in Yorkshire, and Henry VIII lived there with Katharine of Aragon. Elizabeth I, born at Greenwich Palace, died at Richmond Palace.

Flood tide at Richmond (*opposite*). The fisherman is unperturbed and no doubt knows, from his tide-table, when the water will go down again. In recent years, however, flooding of London by the tidal Thames has taken on a grim significance because the land-level is steadily falling and high tides are becoming higher. (*See* pages 16 and 120.)

The Georgian village of Isleworth. The inn on the
left is the London Apprentice. In the 17th and 18th
centuries Isleworth was in the London 'commuter
belt', that is to say it was within easy reach of the City
for merchants who preferred to live up-river, whereas
villages like Kensington were sometimes cut off in
winter because they lacked the advantage of river
communication, and the mud made the
roads impassable.

Syon House, Brentford. In the early 17th century James I gave it to the Earl of Northumberland, and it has remained a home of the Percy family ever since. The exterior was refaced in 1825. Chief of its many splendours are the Robert Adam interiors, notably the Great Hall. Syon has always been known for its gardens, though John Evelyn in 1665 wrote that the house was 'faire enough' but 'more celebrated for the garden than it deserves'. Modern visitors to the gardens are unlikely to share Evelyn's opinion. The rose gardens alone cover six acres. The present park and gardens are largely as designed for the first Duke by Capability Brown, whose boat-house is a reminder that for 1,000 years living near the Thames had the same attraction for the rich and the great as living near M4 has today.

Kew Palace, also known as the Dutch House, was
built in 1631 by a Dutch merchant, Samuel Fortrey.
George III liked to stay here with his large family
during the summer, leading the quiet life of a country
gentleman. In winter the house was particularly cold,
as we know from the complaints of the novelist and
diarist, Fanny Burney, who was keeper of the robes to
Queen Charlotte.

Royal Botanic Gardens, Kew: the Great Palm House,
by Richard Turner and Decimus Burton, 1844–8.
The Gardens were originally made up from two
adjoining royal gardens: that of Kew House, where
Sir Willian Chambers designed the orangery and the
'Chinese' pagoda; and that of Richmond Lodge,
where Capability Brown made the Long Lake.
However, it was not until 1840 that the combined
Royal Botanic Gardens were set up under Sir Joseph
Hooker. Besides delighting millions of visitors, from
London and elsewhere, the Gardens have remained
pre-eminent in the fields of education and research.

Brentford Lock on the Grand Union Canal (*below*).
Nearby the canal and River Brent enter the Thames
a short distance below Syon House. The ford from
which the place takes its name has vanished from sight,
but a granite column records the military importance
of Brentford. Here, it is claimed, the tribesmen
unsuccessfully opposed a Roman crossing of the
Thames in 54 BC; Edmond Ironside, more successfully,
fought the Danes in 1016; and the Royalists defeated
the Parliamentarians during the Civil War.

Strand-on-the-Green. (*opposite, top*). The best-
preserved of all Tideway villages. Its disadvantage is
indicated by the forestair; houses here are frequently
flooded by the ever-rising Thames. (*See* pages 14–15.)
Zoffany lived and painted for twenty years in what is
now Zoffany House, and there are two excellent
pubs: the Bull's Head and the 15th-century City Barge.

Lower Mall, Hammersmith (*opposite, bottom*). This is
part of the rowing man's Tideway; the raft in the
foreground is for launching racing craft, and on
the right is the headquarters of the Amateur
Rowing Association.

The Oxford and Cambridge Boat Race (*below*),
first held at Henley in 1829, has since 1845 been
rowed from Putney to Mortlake over a distance of
4¼ miles. The winding course allows the leading
crew to take its opponent's water and thus add to
its advantage; close finishes are therefore rare.
Nevertheless the University Boat Race continues
to attract immense numbers of spectators. In this
race, in 1975, Cambridge, almost out of the picture,

The Boathouses on Putney Hard (*right*). Here is the
rowing stronghold on the Tideway; among the clubs
are the great, long-established rivals, London Rowing
Club, which celebrated its 125th anniversary in 1981,
and Thames Rowing Club; other notable boathouses
are those of Vesta and of Westminster School. The
balconies of the clubs command fine views of the
start of the University Boat Race and of the finish of
the Head of the River Race, a time-race rowed over
the same course but from Mortlake to Putney, on a
falling tide. In the 'Head', 420 crews, from all over
Britain and from abroad, take part.

River of the 1930s. Gilbert Scott's Battersea Power Station (1932) beyond Chelsea Bridge (1934).

Chelsea Pensioners (*above*). Wren's magnificent
Royal Hospital, opened in 1692, was founded by
Charles II 'out of a tender and deep compassion for
the sad and deplorable condition of many loial and
brave men' – former soldiers.

Doggett's Coat and Badge (*right*). In 1715 Thomas
Doggett, an actor, offered a 'livery with a badge
representing Liberty to be rowed for by six watermen
from London Bridge to Chelsea, annually on the
same day, August 1, for ever'. There were then
perhaps 10,000 watermen on London's river. Now
there are few; but the race is still held.

Houseboats on the Thames at Chelsea (*opposite*).
Some of those who live in the boats presumably do so
because they cannot afford houses or flats of their own
in this area. Yet only a few generations ago, Chelsea
was a cheap place for artists and writers. The list of
those who lived in or near Cheyne Walk, just behind
these boats, is formidable. A few are Whistler, Wilson
Steer, Hilaire Belloc, Carlyle, Kingsley and
Dante Gabriel Rosetti.

The Palace of Westminster (*left*) seen across the river from outside Lambeth Palace. The original Palace of Westminster, except for Westminster Hall, was destroyed by fire in 1834. The rebuilding, finished in 1852, was entrusted, after public competition, to Charles Barry, who brought in Pugin to design much of the detail.

Lambeth Palace (*above*). Archbishops of Canterbury have lived here, only a short row across the river from the King's Palace at Westminster, since the 12th century, and the building is, together with the Tower, one of London's major medieval survivals. The 13th-century Great Hall now houses the library. The Gatehouse seen here dates from 1495.

The Embankment from Waterloo Bridge (*opposite*).
The ship in the foreground, Captain Scott's *Discovery*,
has now been moved to St Katharine's Dock. (*See*
page 117.) The other ships are HMS *Wellington*,
HMS *Chrysanthemum* and HMS *President*. In the
background are St Pauls and the tower block of the
National Westminster Bank.

The Royal Festival Hall (*above*). The major group of
public buildings devoted to the arts, built on the
south bank of the Thames near Waterloo Bridge,
presented architects from the 1950s to the 1970s with
an opportunity seldom equalled. The opportunity
has generally been missed, with buildings that are
functional but not pleasant. However, Robert
Matthew's Royal Festival Hall, of 1951, pleases the
eyes of Londoners as much as its concerts delight
their ears. The Festival Hall makes an effective
contribution to the riverside by night as well as by day.

Fishmongers' Hall (*above*), by London Bridge. The
Fishmongers, one of the great livery companies of the
City of London, have had a Hall here since the reign
of Edward III. The present building dates from
1831–4. Sadly, it is beginning to be overshadowed by
taller neighbours. The Company, which still holds
responsibilities concerned with fisheries, administers
the race for the Doggett's Coat and Badge (page 107),
and on grand occasions Doggett's winners line the
staircase of the Hall.

(*Top*) Memorial in Postmen's Park, Aldersgate.

The Tower of London. William the Conqueror
built the Tower, where Romans and Saxons had
built before him, to dominate the Thames approaches
and to overawe the Londoners. When the historian
John Stow wrote his *Survey of London*, 1598–1603, he
described the Tower as Palace, Treasury, Armoury,
Mint and Prison. Today it is one of the major show-
pieces in London; it is also the best-preserved example
of medieval defensive architecture in Britain.

Tower Bridge from Tower Wharf (*left*). The bridge, with its two bascules which open for river traffic, was built in 1894 by Sir John Wolfe Barry and Isambard Brunel the younger. On royal birthdays and other state occasions salutes are fired from Hyde Park by the King's Troop, RHA, and from this wharf by the Honourable Artillery Company. They use modern guns, however, not those shown here.

Warehouses in the Pool of London (*above*). Many of the warehouses that line the river in the area of the old docks, now fallen into disuse (*see* pages 12–14), have been recognised not only to be well designed for their original purpose, but to be fine buildings, like these, which it would be a pity to pull down. Strenuous efforts are being made to find new uses for them, such as conversion into flats and studios.

St Anne's, Limehouse (*left*); one of Hawksmoor's three churches in the East End, finished in 1726. Limehouse, where the Regent's Canal joins the Thames, connecting the Port of London with the Grand Union Canal and the industrial Midlands, was thought of by Victorians as a sinister district, and is portrayed as such by Dickens in *Our Mutual Friend*. It was probably never as bad as it was painted. St Anne's remains a busy parish church, though most of the small houses have been replaced by high blocks of flats.

Looking down-river towards Tower Bridge (*below*). Lying just above the bridge is the Second World War cruiser, HMS *Belfast*, launched in 1938 and now converted into a floating museum of recent naval history.

St Katharine's Dock (*opposite*). This dock, built by Thomas Telford in 1828, fell out of use in the late 1960s with the coming of container traffic (*see* page 14) but has now been given a new lease of life as a yacht harbour, surrounded by a hotel, flats, the World Trade Centre and many amenities. In the dock lie Captain Scott's ship, *Discovery*, and the *Nore* lightship.

The Painted Hall at Greenwich (*below*). The Royal Naval Hospital (which later became the Royal Naval College) was intended, when Wren began work on it at the end of the 17th century, to be a sailors' counterpart to the soldiers' Royal Hospital, Chelsea (page 107). Wren's Baroque exuberance in the architecture of the dining hall is matched by Thornhill's ceiling, described by Pevsner as 'perhaps the most effective piece of Baroque painting by any English artist'.

The river front of the Royal Naval College, Greenwich (*opposite, top*). Before it was rebuilt in the reign of William and Mary as the Royal Naval Hospital, there had been a royal palace here since the 15th century, the palace of Placentia.

Looking towards the river from the Old Royal Observatory, Greenwich (*opposite, bottom*). Nearest the river is the Royal Naval College; nearer the camera is the National Maritime Museum with, at the centre of the colonnades, the Queen's House, the first Palladian house in England, built by Inigo Jones for James I's queen, Anne of Denmark.

The Thames Barrier (*opposite*) at Woolwich. The
Barrier became necessary because sea-levels all round
Britain have been gradually rising, and particularly in
the south-east. This led to a danger of flooding over a
large area of London, particularly if a very high tide
in spring or autumn co-incides with a tidal surge,
caused by a gale driving sea-water up the funnel of
the Thames Estuary. (*See* page 16.)

The National Data Buoy at Blackwall Yard (*above*).
The buoy was built here in 1975/6 for the Department
of Industry, to collect information on such subjects as
waves, currents, winds and air- and water-
temperatures at sea. After commissioning, it was
moored in the Atlantic for eighteen months,
followed by four years in the North Sea. Blackwall
Yard has been engaged in shipbuilding and marine
engineering since the 16th century and is now active
in North Sea oil development.

Woolwich: the Rotunda (*above*). Woolwich is rich in fine buildings, most of them designed for army use, such as the Royal Military Academy and the Royal Artillery Barracks. The Rotunda, less obviously military, was designed by John Nash as a temporary pavilion for the Prince Regent in St James's Park in 1814. After Waterloo it was rebuilt at Woolwich as a permanent structure, and housed some of the spoils of victory. In the 1970s it was restored, and is now a museum of the evolution of the gun from Crecy to the present day.

Cooling Marshes (*below*), on the Kentish shore, west
of the Isle of Grain. Here the land has changed little
for many centuries, and the sheep graze undisturbed.
The Romney Marsh breed, known as Kents outside
the Romney area, remain the type best suited to the
conditions. Nearby is Cooling Castle, built in 1382.
The castle, and the 14th-century parish church,
suggest that these marshlands were rich when wealth
came from agriculture and not from industry or oil.

Southend-on-Sea (*below*). Southend began life as an 18th-century oyster fishery, but became a holiday town after the Prince Regent made sea-bathing fashionable. In the 19th century and early decades of this century it was a popular seaside resort within easy reach of day-trippers from the East End of London, by train or charabanc. It still retains its hold, as the picture indicates; and it has managed to keep many attractive buildings from the opening decades of the 19th century.

The Isle of Grain oil refinery (*opposite*), just east of Cooling Marshes. The refinery was opened by BP in the 1950s, taking crude from Iran and other Middle East sources and more recently from the North Sea, and refining it to provide petrol, diesel fuel, aviation fuel, heating and industrial fuels and lubricants, and tar for roads. In 1981 the decision was taken to close the refinery because demand for industrial fuels had fallen. Sheep (*see* page 123) continued to graze close to the refinery, and even inside it, though they then became distinctly black sheep.

Dry dock at Sheerness (*left*), Isle of Sheppey. The naval dockyard at Sheerness was built in the early 19th century by Rennie, but in 1960 the Admiralty decided to close it, and it was bought by a consortium of investors. It was seen to have great potential as a commercial port because, in addition to the naval installations, it claims to have the deepest harbour between the Firth of Forth and Milford Haven.

Thames Sailing Barges (*below*). These flat-bottomed barges, with leeboards for tacking, were highly successful in coastal trade because they could be sailed by 'one man and a boy', carried some 200 tons, and could be beached on a falling tide and unloaded by horse and cart. Nowadays a number of them are kept going by enthusiastic admirers.

Queenborough Church, Isle of Sheppey (*opposite*). The town takes its name from Queen Philippa, wife of Edward III. Edward built the town in the late 14th century, together with a castle, to command the Medway estuary. The castle has gone, and the church bears little sign of its royal origins. The name Sheppey means 'island of sheep'.

Author's Acknowledgements

A. P. Herbert once remarked that there are almost as many books about
the Thames as there are about love. For those in search of further
reading, and whose appetite may have been wetted by this brief
pictorial survey, the standard work is still F. S. Thacker's *The Thames
Highway*, Vol I 1914, Vol II 1920, republished in 1968 by David and
Charles. The best modern work is J. R. L. Anderson's *The Upper
Thames*, Eyre and Spottiswoode, 1970. That book includes an
extensive bibliography, and indeed contains everything else that the
general reader is likely to need, within the geographical limits set by
the title. For an account of recent improvements on the Tideway I can
recommend John Doxat's *The Living Thames* by Hutchinson Benham.

I am indebted to the Editor of *Country Life* for permission to reprint
material from an article by myself, *The Lost World of London's
Watermen*, first published on November 15, 1979, and to Oxford
University Press for allowing me to use the three verses from
J. D. C. Pellow's poem; to Patricia Pierce and Margaret Saunders, of
Country Life Books, for unfailing help and advice in choosing and
captioning the pictures; and to Mike Hall and Dr John Banks of the
Thames Water Authority, and John McArthur of the Port of London
Authority, for much information and for submitting to my many
questions. I have also drawn from papers read at a seminar held by the
River Thames Society at Marlow in October, 1978. The Society
deserves the support of all who love the river; the address of its
administrative office is 2 Chestnut Lodge Cottages, Old Common
Road, Cobham, Surrey. The address of the Thames Heritage Trust, set
up in 1979 to co-ordinate the efforts of the many public bodies and
private organisations concerned with the welfare and future of the
Thames, is Gresham House, Twickenham Road, Feltham, Middlesex.

Illustration Acknowledgements

John Bethel, St Albans 19, 24–25, 32 bottom, 50, 52, 53, 54–55,
55 top, 62, 74, 76–77, 88, 88–89, 91, 92, 98, 101 top, 101 bottom, 110,
117, 118; British Tourist Authority, London 46, 66–67, 75, 102,
107 top; J. Allan Cash, London 35, 60–61, 69, 81, 107 bottom;
Colorsport, London 79; Colour Library International, London 2, 7,
8–9, 30–31, 32 top, 34, 40–41, 45, 49 bottom, 51, 60, 64–65, 66, 68–69,
71, 72–73, 82, 87, 90, 93 bottom, 97, 104–105, 108, 109, 111, 112
bottom, 113, 114, 119 top, 119 bottom, 126 top; W. F. Davidson,
Penrith 23; Michael Dent, Richmond 95, 96–97, 126 bottom; Greg
Evans, London 63; André Goulancourt, Ashford, Middlesex 58;
Greater London Council 120; Hamlyn Group Picture Library 93 top;
Brian Hawkes, Newnham 18, 122–123, 125; Angelo Hornak,
London 116 top, 122; The Institute of Oceanographic Services,
Godalming 121; A. F. Kersting, London 46–47, 48–49, 56–57, 70
bottom, 84–85; Andrew Lawson, Charlbury 20–21, 21 top, 21 bottom,
22, 26, 26–27, 28, 29 bottom, 30 top, 30 bottom, 32–33, 36, 37, 38, 39,
42, 44, 49 top, 56, 70 top; S. & O. Matthews, Godstone 59 top, 112 top,
124, 127; National Trust, London 55 bottom; Patricia Pierce,
Sunbury-on-Thames 100; Mike Roberts, Greenford 78, 80, 83, 84, 86,
94, 106; M. Saunders, London 99; Spectrum Colour Library, London
13–14, 43, 59 bottom; Homer Sykes, London 76; Thames and
Chilterns Tourist Board, Abingdon 29 top; J. Todd, London 102–103;
ZEFA – Handford 14–15, 116 bottom; ZEFA – Bert Leichmann 115.